THE WELL-SPRINGS OF PRAYER

Joy be with you always. Never cease praying. Give thanks upon all occasions; this is what God expects of you all in Christ Jesus.

1 *Thess.* 5, 16-18

THE WELL-SPRINGS OF PRAYER

by

DOM GEORGES LEFEBVRE, O.S.B.

DESCLEE COMPANY

NEW YORK · TOURNAI · PARIS · ROME 1961

This book was first published in France, under the title *La Grâce de la prière* by Desclée de Brouwer et cie, in 1958. The translation into English was made by Kathleen Pond.

The translator would like to thank the Rev. F. F. Taylor for drawing this work to her notice, and for the encouragement he has given in its translation.

Nihil obstat Hubertus Richards S.T.L., L.S.S.,
Censor deputatus
Imprimatur E. Morrogh Bernard, *Vic. Gen.*
Westmonasterii, die 11° Julii, 1960.

The *Nihil obstat* and *Imprimatur* are a declaration that a book or pamphlet is considered to be free from doctrinal or moral error. It is not implied that those who have granted the *Nihil obstat* and *Imprimatur* agree with the contents, opinions or statements expressed.

Library of Congress Catalogue Card No. 61744

Made and printed in Great Britain in 1960.

CONTENTS

FOREWORD

I want in this book to set down in an immediately practical form an idea of prayer, which is the inspiration of the whole of the spiritual life. I should like these pages to be able to support the soul in prayer, to help it to pray in an atmosphere of recollection and of the presence of God.

So you will find here simply a sequence of short passages which express the fundamental attitudes of the soul in prayer or, rather, certain aspects of the attitude of prayer which is basically a single whole but which can be more readily grasped if we look one by one at the various strands which go to make it up.

I hope that what I have written will help to create the atmosphere of prayer.

I have given, by way of introduction and before specifying their exact meaning and bearing, a few general remarks on prayer.

PRAYER

'The Union of Simplicity and Purity'

—*St. John of the Cross.*

PRAYER

IN EVERY soul sanctified by grace God dwells and the Blessed Trinity is actively present, infusing it with new life and the power to enter into communion with the three divine Persons and to share in the mystery of their love.

Prayer means keeping oncsclf in this presence and responding to its life-giving influence. It means being responsive to grace, whose work in our souls is uninterrupted, whether its action can in some sense be perceived or remains entirely hidden. For the divine reality will always be infinitely beyond what we are able to grasp of it in fleeting glimpses and if we do attain to true, deep contact with God, it will only be through trying to respond to grace in an attitude of humble submissiveness.

It is for this reason that prayer is primarily an attitude of the will. The soul must be turned towards God and seek him; it must be a soul of desire, responsive to grace. This attitude consists in a few simple dispositions which will be found over and over again in the spiritual life, the pattern of which they form.

The sentiments we never tire of expressing to God do not vary, but gradually we come to clothe them in another form. At the outset we endeavoured to foster such sentiments as much as we could by our own efforts, that by so doing we might find ourselves able to live more fully by grace. But as its hold over us becomes more marked, grace impregnates the soul so deeply with these aspirations that eventually it reaches the point at which nothing more is needed than to allow them to well up from its inmost recesses as a pure gift of God.

Considered in its essence, prayer is a unity. It is the life of grace expanding and, through its inspirations, gradually taking possession of the soul. In the beginning, however, this life is only in us as an embryo which has not yet developed all its potentialities. We are scarcely aware of the fundamental tendencies with which it has marked the soul. At this point such tendencies are only beginning to come to life and their action on the heart's movements, however real, is still as it were blurred and difficult for us to perceive. It is nevertheless these tendencies that we are already searching after in prayer and the purpose of the work of meditation is to help us to discover them. If they do not yet make themselves felt sufficiently strongly to draw us to recollection, at least if we make an effort to enter into ourselves we become aware of the first stirrings of these divine instincts which grace has implanted in our souls. If we occupy ourselves with thoughts which keep our attention in this direction, we will become aware that there is something within us which responds to these aspirations and is in harmony with them. The response will at times be very subdued but gradually, as St Gertrude so aptly expresses it, the soul trains its ear to catch the hushed whisper of divine love.

Acquired habit and, at the same time, the increasing intervention of grace in our effort will gradually allow us to catch this whisper more clearly. And so the moment will come when the soul is called to a more hidden and silent prayer; it is all important to recognize this moment. The danger, moreover (many a quotation from St John of the Cross would show that this was his view also) would seem to be not so much in abandoning meditation too quickly—boredom and the emptiness of total inaction would probably cure us of this illusion quickly enough; the danger seems rather to be in not being able to recognize the operation of grace when it begins to work in our soul. For this grace is hidden. The blessings it brings are 'invisible blessings', a peace 'which the soul does not perceive'.

These expressions are taken from St John of the Cross, whose teaching on this point is so absolutely and unquestionably definitive that it is not possible to touch on this question without quoting him.

In the first place it should be recalled that there is no question of making a permanent choice, of determining one particular moment when, having passed through one stage, we should give up one particular form of prayer once and for all to take up another that is simpler and more perfect.[1] Particularly in the first stages, we shall be drawn at one time to remain in deeper silence before God, at another to do more by our own efforts to seek him out, to go forth to meet him; it is important to become submissive to this guidance of grace through our

[1] On this point see *Ascent of Mount Carmel*, Bk. II, ch. 15.

constant care always to adapt our response to God's call.

To help us in this matter St John of the Cross has given us three signs by which the interior call to a simpler form of prayer can be recognized. Moreover in a certain sense these signs may all be reduced to the third. But since this third sign is of itself somewhat difficult to discern, we must frequently turn to the other two in order to be quite certain that the third is present.

'The third and surest sign is that the soul takes pleasure in being alone and waits with loving attentiveness upon God without making any particular meditation, in inward peace, quietness and rest . . . the soul is alone with an attentiveness and a knowledge, general and loving' (*Ascent of Mount Carmel*, Bk. II, ch.13[1]). 'But here it must be made clear that this general knowledge whereof we are speaking is at all times so subtle and delicate—particularly when it is most pure, simple and perfect, most spiritual and most interior—that although the soul be occupied therein, it can neither realize nor perceive it' (Chap. 14).

Put very simply, this is an inner silence in which the soul feels drawn to remain in peace. Its effects are wholly good. The soul feels at ease. It seems to us that in this silence we are receiving a hidden but strengthening food. It may happen, however, that despite the great attraction to enter this silence, as soon as the soul withdraws into it, it seems empty, and we think we are

---

[1] This and other quotations from St. John of the Cross are taken from the translation of E. Allison Peers. (Burns, Oates and Washbourne, Ltd., London 1934.)

remaining there in idleness. It is then that the other two signs must be tested.

The first point is that if we wish to return to our ordinary practice of meditation we find it impossible to do so and something calls us to recollection in peace and tranquillity. This is the first 'sign which the spiritual person will find in himself . . . that he can no longer meditate or reason with his imagination, as he was wont to do aforetime' (Chap. 13). Not only do we no longer find profit in 'thus reasoning with the imagination', but if in spite of everything we try to attempt this, we feel we cannot, that something is preventing us. It is as if we were trying to converse with someone in order to take our attention off what another person, to whom we cannot entirely avoid listening, is saying.

To this sign will be added another: 'the second sign is a realization that he has no desire to fix his meditation or his mind upon any particular object, exterior or interior. I do not mean that the imagination neither comes nor goes (for it is wont to move freely, even at times of great recollection), but that the soul has no pleasure in fixing it deliberately upon any object' (Chap. 13). 'The imaginative faculty in this state of recollection is in the habit of coming and going and varying of its own accord, but neither according to the pleasure nor at the will of the soul, which is troubled thereby because its peace and joy are disturbed' (Chap. 14).

Thus we may find ourselves overwhelmed with distractions which, without depriving us of the almost imperceptible foundation of peace and interior calm, will nevertheless draw us away in all directions; St John of the Cross even says that it is 'the custom' of the imagination to seek to escape from the recollection in which the soul dwells through its higher faculties. If, however, it tries to think of anything voluntarily, or deliberately to fix the attention on one or other of these distractions, it finds it cannot do so, but is at once repelled by all this and drawn into its innermost centre by this need of silence and peace. For although imagination may roam as it pleases, the will cannot try to follow it without feeling itself interiorly pulled back by the grace which keeps it secretly but firmly fixed in God.

To try to fix one's thoughts voluntarily on a particular object may even be a means of recognizing the call of grace. We then feel that something is drawing us within, that it would be painful and cause a certain suffering and distress to leave our inward recollection and concentrate on something else.

When this call comes, it is important that the soul should be submissive to it. We must be willing to efface ourselves so as to leave, as St John of the Cross says, 'all the room for God' (Chap. 5). It is not, however, that we no longer have to act, only that now we must do so in a different manner. Our collaboration is still necessary. True, God is the master and he can, if he pleases, take possession of a soul so forcefully that he seems, as it were, to take hold of it in spite of itself. This, however, can only be an exceptional case. Normally we have a part in making ourselves responsive to God's action in us, in surrendering to it—at the very least we must turn aside from the various preoccupations which clamour for our attention, and establish ourselves in that interior silence to which grace calls us, though it does not force us to accept the call.

This effort of attention will perhaps be something scarcely perceptible. Caught up by grace and effacing ourselves in grace, we seem to be doing nothing and to be wholly passive, and yet, however gently and simply, we must surrender ourselves to the work that God is accomplishing in us.

The truth is that the result thus obtained, namely the attitude of recollection in which we find ourselves, is the fruit of grace, and that we could not achieve anything of the kind by our own resources.

So, in whatever way it is asked of us to collaborate with the action of grace, we must always, in one way or another, see that we are responsive to it. We can help to elicit this response by making use of a few simple phrases which will serve merely to remind us in different ways of the attitude that forms the basis of our endeavour to remain in the presence of God—an interior attitude which seems to be in close harmony with the truths the faith teaches us. We know that, explicitly or not, it is by them that we live and that outside these truths our prayer would no longer have any basis and would lose all its meaning.

Through this effort to become aware of the divine realities we bear within us there will gradually be awakened an attraction for a deeper prayer, a desire to see the interior dispositions through which the presence of these realities becomes known to us and strengthens their hold over our hearts. Moreover, in the very desire to belong more completely to God there is something of the unconditional gift, a beginning, indeed, of the perfect prayer of a soul that is completely surrendered to him.

Such an offering is acceptable before God.

The following pages seek to promote and sustain such an effort towards prayer.

SUBMISSION TO GRACE

I

THE LIFE OF GRACE

PRECISELY IN the measure in which we strive to do everything by our own efforts do we suffer from our own helplessness. Obstacles from every side seem to us to impede our upward movement towards God. We remain confined within our own limitations, which we are incapable of transcending, while we feel that the goal we are pursuing is remote. We are like an insect continually hurtling itself against a pane of glass, until the day we discover the only way of escaping from ourselves and soaring freely towards God—the way of faith in the free gift of grace, grace in the face of which the inadequacy of our efforts is abundantly clear, but which it is so simple to accept as a gift.

Since everything in us is the work of the free gift of grace, the way to live more deeply by this grace is not to strive to see its effects more clearly, but something much simpler—to consent to receive everything as God's free gift, accepting the complete stripping of ourselves that that presupposes and keeping ourselves in an attitude of simplicity and interior freedom by which we express our confidence in him on whom we depend for everything.

Union with God is a mutual gift, which is why its effect is to give the soul with increasing intensity the impression of living in the presence of God in an atmosphere of freedom.

The interior dispositions of which we are aware in ourselves are the fruit of sancifying grace and the expression of its deepest tendencies. Our whole life of prayer rests on this essential gift. We cannot live by this gift without finding ourselves in an atmosphere of simplicity, of joy freely given, of thanksgiving, of calm and confident humility.

In the very liberty that we enjoy in prayer, in the simplicity with which we turn to God in expectation of his grace, is expressed the realization that we have of receiving everything from him.

We stand before God in the simplest attitude we can assume in his presence, and we know ourselves to be in that presence because we find ourselves in an attitude that it is possible to assume only before him.

Our prayer is the interior disposition which has gradually been established in us by the action of grace. For such prayer to become actualized, all that is necessary is that this interior attitude should come to the surface, however slightly, and for that no more is needed than a mere desire in which we turn to God. The very least act will suffice to elicit this prayer which is dormant in us.

Even if we feel that we are doing nothing and all within us seems emptiness, we know that in this silence

God is present, accomplishing in us the work of his grace, and that the peace which we find in this complete self-effacement is a sufficient sign for us that, despite appearances, we are attentive to the divine presence.

If we find ourselves in a state of complete dryness, we have only to accept our poverty and denudation with the simplicity and freedom we can derive from the realization that we are living by the gifts of God.

We have no need to see the effects of God's goodness in ourselves. We believe in his divine goodness and this simple act of faith is the basis of our whole interior attitude. We simply remain in an inward silence which in itself is an attitude of submission. It is sufficient for us to know that such an attitude opens the soul to the action of grace. True, this remains hidden from us, but were this not so we should not experience in the same way the joy of being in God's hands, wholly dependent on his bounty.

Austere as it can be, the inner silence in which we remain so to speak in a disposition of dependence and submission is not painful or difficult. The very simple joy found in this state is proof that we realize that what we are submitting to is for our good, that the submission is an act of confidence and gratitude—of deeper dependence on God.

We have only to keep silence to find within ourselves that which we should receive as one does a gift, that is, just as it is given. To realize that we live by the gifts of God is to leave the choice of those gifts to him.

It is not a question of our putting ourselves in an interior attitude of our own choosing, of which we should have to form a precise idea for ourselves in order to be able to adopt it. It is a matter of allowing God to put us, by grace, in the attitude he wants for us, and for this we have only to turn towards him as simply as possible, in a disposition of expectancy and of complete surrender. We have simply to be attuned to grace, whose work in us is none other than to make us increasingly responsive. God himself, acting in us, makes us submissive to his work in us. All we have to do is to allow him to make us submissive and give ourselves up to his work in us.

In this disposition which wells up in us, we experience something which comes not from ourselves but from grace. We realize that to submit to this is to become pliable in God's hands and from this our whole joy arises.

II

JOY

There is joy in living by grace, in living by the gifts of God. We become aware that we are living by a gift, living gratuitously. From this comes our joy, a joy wholly impregnated with the need of recognizing that all we have we have received.

It is a joy that is completely pure, because completely gratuitous, a joy so pure and delicate that it is scarcely perceptible to us. We are merely aware that we are living in simplicity and interior freedom.

We feel we cannot penetrate to the depths of this joy, for it springs from a reality that remains hidden from us. We do not know why we are so happy and this shows us how completely this happiness is a sheer gift, since we possess it without even being able to say whence it comes. We are content simply to enjoy it and this very simplicity is the expression of the humility filled with confidence with which we desire to receive this joy which comes from God and remains his and his alone.

It is a joy which is based on an act of faith. We enjoy a happiness which remains hidden from us but of which we know that it is scaled to the measure of God's goodness and of his love for us. If we love this joy so deeply, it is because we see in it a gift of God's goodness to us.

We have only to follow the attraction of this interior joy to make the sacrifices demanded of us, simply and spontaneously, without attaching too much importance to what they cost us, without letting our thoughts dwell on them, without losing our serenity, for we continue to remain fundamentally happy.

The sign of the presence of this hidden joy in the soul is the fact that we no longer experience any desire which we cannot renounce without losing our peace.

The fruit of this interior joy is the desire to give joy, to show to others the same loving kindness that God is bestowing on us. We should strive always to see in our neighbour someone to whom we owe his share of the joy which God has given us.

Our conviction that we receive all we have as a free gift inspires us with the desire to give ourselves completely in return.

It is the loving-kindness of a soul that is truly happy, a kindness which radiates from its joy and which is in exact proportion to its joy.

III

HUMILITY

Our disposition is primarily one of joy, joy that is very simple but which brings complete peace because we find ourselves in possession of a good which satisfies us completely and which we cannot but enjoy more, in proportion as our aspirations become purer. What makes the purity of this joy, however, is that it is a given happiness, a gift of God which can only be received in a heart sufficiently detached from itself and all it possesses, to live solely by the gifts of God in the attitude of poverty and of entire dependence that that presupposes.

The deepest tendencies of the soul, which were formerly turned in upon itself, are now, so to speak, drawn elsewhere. The desire for self-assertion is changed into a great need of dependence and submission. Our joy now is to remain before God in the realization of our poverty. We learn to love humility, to consider it as our only good.

Our only good may be said to be the disposition to

humiliate and submit ourselves and this is the fruit of grace in us and establishes us in a state of detachment which forms our whole prayer.

The prayer becomes more perfect in the measure in which it becomes, more truly and sincerely, the expression of interior surrender, the self-stripping of a soul who is conscious of receiving everything from the wholly gratuitous goodness of God.

To keep one's peace in the midst of complete interior detachment is the attitude of a humble and submissive soul that is stripped of self, and is a perfect prayer. We then feel our poverty and humility and that everything in us is becoming calmer, more flexible and responsive.

The more the action of God in us remains hidden, the more we live in the realization that we hold everything from him alone, a realization which makes us increasingly humble and submissive.

The work of grace is a work of detachment. Through aridity and interior humiliations, we gradually find ourselves established in a state in which we are stripped to the very bone; the realization of our poverty and helplessness detaches us from self. At the same time we feel that this is bringing us untold good. In this crushing of self we experience a peace which gives us the assurance that we are not being left to our own wretchedness, but that we are in the hands of God who is watching over us with infinite loving kindness.

Thus in the depths of our lowliness we find—and it can be found nowhere else—a joy that is all the purer and more delicate for being hidden and utterly detached, the joy of receiving everything as a gift, the joy of a love that is entirely gratuitous.

We are then established in an interior disposition of humility and joy and these two sentiments combine to form an attitude of serenity in the face of every circumstance. To have an attitude of calmness in every circumstance in this way is the sign that we are truly detached and the mark of the highest perfection.

The soul finds delight in this humility and it has a softening influence on everything within it.

Humility brings more blessings than any other virtue. Wherever it is, it leaves behind it an impression of calm and peace. It is the soul's friend. It does us good delicately, gently, making all within us simpler and more peaceful and diffusing a secret joy which is hidden but utterly pure.

We are at peace and calm because we are sincerely humble. This peace is wholly made up of humility.

It is humility which makes a heart pure and truly detached, which gives it that inward delicacy of self-forgetfulness and effacement which enables it to enter into friendship with God.

We realize how truly God is all and that is why we take delight in receiving all things from him gratuitously. Everything seems worthless to us except what comes from him and anything we can draw from our own depths seems to us sheer nothingness. Realizing our own nothingness, the nothingness of every thought and wish that come from self, we cannot but remain in entire submissiveness to God, loving nothing but his will alone.

We feel our utter poverty, but it is in this very poverty that we put our trust, for we know that nothing can prevent God from doing what he wills in souls that no longer possess anything of their own.

Our deeply-rooted inclination to humble ourselves and be submissive is simply an attitude of the spirit of faith. The better we understand the supernatural character of our life, which is a pure gift of God, the better we shall understand that we can do nothing of ourselves, but only through humble submission to God's action in us.

IV

SUBMISSION

We offer ourselves to God in all simplicity, placing ourselves completely at his disposal. We simply surrender to the need for entire submission and this produces in us the realization that all we receive is a free gift from God's generosity. This submission is a joyful thing, for what we are submitting to is our own blessed good. More than a submission, it is the realization that we no longer belong to ourselves, that we are not in our own hands, that we depend entirely on God who gives us life by his gifts.

In the depths of our being we can always find at least this attitude of humble and confident submission which does not depend on our own will, but is in us as an effect of the loving-kindness with which God surrounds us.

It is impossible to live by God's gifts and enjoy this atmosphere of complete gratuitousness in which we find ourselves in his presence without feeling the need to strip ourselves of the only thing that is our own, our will. The sign that we are so stripped is when in our relations with our neighbour no assertion of our own will appears.

There are in the soul two wills—the will that finds itself drawn in all directions by all kinds of human affairs and whose advance is painful, soiled as it is with the dust of the road. These imperfect sentiments cannot be completely silenced, but the soul will find peace only in the measure in which it allows the other will to emerge—that which disregarding itself once and for all, now allows God and God alone to will for it.

Thus two possible attitudes may arise when a sacrifice has to be made—that of the soul who makes an effort to give up something of what is its own; that of the soul who no longer has anything of its own and allows God to take from it freely.

To submit to God's will is to move away from our personal preoccupations, from our petty, selfish outlook, to enter another order of reality in which everything is beyond our personal capacity and must be left in God's hands.

The will of God is not a will alien from our own. It is our own will's most intimate life. Our will cannot expand or be fully itself except by adhering to God's will with every fibre of its being.

To submit to God is no longer to have any will but that of living according to his will. It is to allow him to model our will on his. It is to remain open to his grace in all simplicity, to acquiesce in his will with the whole of our being. It is a simple cleaving to God, a simple movement towards him. All that is needed is that this should be true and sincere. Grace penetrates and envelops it on every side.

God respects our liberty. He does not, however, refuse to take it more particularly into his hands if we ourselves ask him. He never abandons to his own weakness anyone who, conscious of that weakness, seeks refuge in a more whole-hearted submissiveness to grace and surrenders to it in an act of humility and confidence, anyone whose sole desire is to allow grace to accomplish in him what he recognizes he is incapable of doing himself.

V

ABANDONMENT

God wraps us round with his wholly gratuitous loving-kindness. It is an atmosphere in which we are conscious of the life within us and this is sufficient for the dispositions which should be ours in the presence of this infinite goodness to well up in us spontaneously—without the need for us to be explicitly aware of them. We feel we are in God's hands and under the protection of his goodness. Of this, at least, we have no doubt. This conviction is the clearest fruit of the working of grace in us, the thing that abides, when all else seems to have left us.

We must live by faith in this divine goodness, not wanting to choose ourselves what seems best, but desiring to receive everything from the hands of God, welcoming all that comes from him as our only good. There is no other happiness for us but the accomplishment of God's infinitely loving plan for us. God is present in our life, accomplishing the plan of his grace. We must allow him freely to realize this work in us which is his and his alone. For our part we should remain simply responsive to his action, in an attitude of humble submissiveness.

We should remain in humble submission to the will of God, simply waiting on its accomplishment in us. In these dispositions we experience a joy full of hope, a deep sense of security, for we have abandoned ourselves to the good pleasure of a will that we know to be nothing but loving-kindness in our regard.

Our joy is to know that we are the object of God's loving will and to realize the utter gratuitousness of this gift. What is of paramount importance for us is the realization that we are living by a wholly gratuitous gift.

SILENCE

I

SIMPLICITY

THE FRUIT of grace is simplicity, a simplicity which opens out into confidence—and it is for that reason that it is the source of joy. It is a simplicity based on humility, which is why the joy it gives is so pure and delicate.

An interior attitude of simplicity and meekness is the natural one for a soul which, no longer having anything of its own, lives by the spirit of gratuitousness which is that of grace.

To be conscious of living by the gifts of God is to have confidence in him from whom we hold all that we have. Thus those who are conscious of living by the free gift of grace cannot be other than wholly simple. They feel they are in an atmosphere of freedom and simplicity. If they lack simplicity it is because they have not yet understood how completely everything in them comes from God.

We sense in an obscure way that this attitude of simplicity is born out of all the dispositions whose growth in us is the work of grace, and we do not feel the need to analyse it in order to discover each of these dispositions individually.

Detachment consists in looking upon all things in the light of this attitude of interior simplicity.

As to the disposition of sincerity, we offer ourselves to God in the sincerity of a very simple gift of self, detached from all those elements of feeling which might involve us in the danger of exaggerating our real interior dispositions to ourselves. A soul can be simple in the measure in which it feels itself truly sincere and the sincerity of our love of God lies in our renouncement of ourselves.

Simplicity is the soul offering itself to God just as it is, that he may do what he pleases with it. It is a gift of self.

Confronted with an actual sacrifice to be made, the soul should act with the same simplicity as in prayer. It is sufficient for us to place ourselves in a very simple attitude of acceptance for the sacrifice thus consented to become the instrument of a movement of grace in us which will strip us of self more completely.

II

DIVINE LIFE

We should prefer a completely simple prayer, such as the humble love to make. It is this very simplicity that makes it pure, and that makes it the expression of our self-effacement in the presence of the mystery of grace which is being wrought in us.

We know that we shall rediscover all the fundamental tendencies of grace, of which we have gradually learnt to become aware in the simplest aspiration towards God which wells up in us, by the very fact that that impulse itself proceeds from an inspiration of grace.

Our simplicity should be that of a soul which is content to know that its least action proceeds from grace and expresses all the life-giving riches of grace—all the riches of a life that is not ours alone, for it is in intimate contact with the life of God and subsists only through its union with this divine life whence it draws its whole existence.

We are content to turn towards God quite simply, content to place under the influence of grace a very simple act, the simplest we can make. It is sufficient that we should thus offer to God our utter willingness for him to do what he pleases with us.

The more we seek to understand our prayer, the more we imprison it within the limits of our own thoughts. On the other hand, the more we are content with a very simple act, the more this act will come under the influence of grace alone and will express all the richness of grace.

We have nothing to offer to God but a very simple act, the simplest we can make, but we know that the whole value of this act comes from the divine gift of grace which is in us and which vivifies our least action. What we offer to God is God's own life which is within us, but the means we have of laying hold of this life in order to offer it, is to place under its influence an act so simple, so tiny, that the offering remains a token of our own weakness and humility.

We can see clearly that our prayer is a gift that we find within ourselves. What we offer to God is something which we find within ourselves, but which we realize does not belong to us. To be able to live by this good that is not our own, we must be content to possess nothing as our own.

The grace by which we live and which ought to be expressed in each one of our actions is not an acquired state in which we are immutably established, it is a life which never ceases to well up and be renewed in us under the influence of the Holy Spirit.

Thus we offer to God not only our actual dispositions at a given moment, we offer ourselves in an attitude of complete responsiveness to the most perfect dispositions that grace seeks to promote in us.

What we find in the depths of our being is not merely an interior disposition which we offer to God as an attitude of adoration and love, but a still deeper and more secret influence of grace which can be glimpsed through the interior disposition which is its fruit; something living and active whose presence transforms everything in us and which we cannot approach without experiencing its influence more deeply.

III

BELIEVING IN GRACE

The soul lives by grace. It has some dim perception of this gift that is hidden within it, but it does not try to lay hold of it through perceptible tokens of its presence. It leaves it in God's hands as his possession, of which he is always free to dispose as he wills. We are content simply to be what we are through the grace that is in us, to keep our eyes open to the light with which God illuminates us, conscious of being utterly dependent on him because of this gift we have received from his wholly gratuitous loving-kindness.

We know by experience that we have within us a divine gift, something which is of God. We could not explain what this treasure is, all we know is that we are enjoying its possession; nor could we explain what the new life is, all we know is that everything in us has become simpler and more peaceful. We do not know why we are in such great peace, but only that all our aspirations are fulfilled. In this peace we seem to possess something infinitely precious which remains hidden from us, a gift of God, a pledge of his loving-kindness towards us.

We feel that there is within us, beyond all that we can perceive, something that is from God, a hidden reality whose secret we must respect, for that is the only way of giving recognition to its character as a divine thing belonging to God alone.

A hidden reality does not mean something more difficult to perceive with the senses, but something which we must give up trying to perceive in the way of the senses, something which is of another order, deeper, more delicate, more secret—a reality which remains hidden, but of which the soul is just sufficiently conscious to be dissatisfied with anything less.

The sign of the presence of divine light in us is that we can no longer be satisfied with any other light. We have caught a glimpse of a deeper reality and can no longer linger over anything, no longer rest in anything, until we have attained it.

The sign that we possess this light is the fact that we are seeking it.

IV

SELF-EFFACEMENT

We are only truly happy in the measure in which, going beyond self, what we find in our inmost depths is no longer ourselves but God. We feel that in our deepest recesses there is a place where we no longer belong to ourselves. When we look into ourselves, all that we find bids us look towards God. We feel that what is closest to us is not our own, and that to live thereby means turning wholly towards him from whom we hold everything. This is simply the attitude of a soul turned towards God, occupied with him alone. We realize that we are living by a life which is in God, and to live now consists for us solely in being drawn towards him.

The life of grace has its own instincts. Realizing that it is a life freely bestowed upon us, we instinctively turn towards him who is its source.

Everything in the soul is now orientated towards God. Every movement which arises in it terminates in an in being drawn towards him.

We have only to keep silence within ourselves to find this silence wholly centred on God. In simplicity, in the deepest recesses of our being, we find a tendency to look towards God which is an indication that we expect everything from him and refer all things to him.

We need only be ourselves, just as we are at the moment we turn towards God. It is by looking on him with simplicity that we feel the effects of his grace beginning to work in us.

We must turn to God with the simplicity of a soul who knows it is in his hands and knows it has not to seek him since he is continually there.

When we look into ourselves we find no longer self, but God; that is why we can no longer refer anything to ourselves. No longer possessing anything of our own, we see only God in our life, a life in which we now look on everything as belonging to God alone.

The sign of the presence of grace in us is a complete detachment from self which can only come from our belonging to God. Our deepest aspirations, as they are turned Godwards, are gradually stripped of any inclination to egoism that was in them.

Prayer is a simple adherence of the soul to this fundamental movement towards God, from which we must not allow ourselves to be turned aside by the will to anything that may be inspired by selfish motives.

Prayer is a simple upward movement of the soul towards God; the only thing that matters is that God should cause it to move out of itself.

We should come to love the will of God sufficiently to lose all regard for our own will and no longer to count that as anything—sufficiently to give up our will without a thought, as a thing of no value.

Progress in self-effacement will be the sign that our deepest inspiration is increasingly turning towards God and that we can thus content ourselves with this prayer of simplicity and can remain in this silence in which everything in us moves spontaneously towards God.

It is through everything of which we see ourselves deprived that we become aware of the action of grace within us. The resistance offered by egoism gradually yields and desires lose their intensity.

The sign of God's presence is all that effaces itself and disappears before him.

When God enlightens us, something turns us aside from our own light and prevents us from clinging to it.

When we are united to God, something turns us aside from our own will and prevents us from taking pleasure in it.

When we no longer find self within our hearts, it is because God is present.

V

SILENCE

The soul must be silent before God. Our attitude should be wholly one of silence, but of silence which is an avowal of our helplessness, of our dependence, silence which is an attitude of humility.

The sign by which we shall be able to recognize that this silence is not pure idleness will be our desire to express in the whole of our life this interior disposition of humility and self-effacement, in particular through the practice of self-forgetfulness and patience in the exercise of charity towards our neighbour.

It is a simple silence, full of the longing for God. It is he whom we seek in this silence and that is why it is a prayer.

It is a silence that is an expectation, the humblest of expectations—the expectation of a gift with the knowledge of its complete gratuitousness.

The soul by its very silence shows that it expects everything from God.

It is a silence that is not only an expectation of, but a response to grace, for it is made up of the dispositions of humility and of submission full of trust, which it fosters in us.

It is simply the silence of the soul in which it senses that that which escapes it as soon as it sets out to seek it, is a hidden thing. We have simply to be ourselves to find springing up spontaneously within us the fundamental tendencies which grace has implanted deep in us.

To pray is to be sincere with ourselves, to find beneath our superficial or artificial inclinations the fundamental tendency of the soul, that by which it lives and which is a grace from God.

Prayer is not only a passing activity. It is the expression of an habitual disposition deeply imprinted upon the soul. It is the expression of its very life, of its deepest tendencies. Its sole preoccupation should be to keep at a distance everything that can distract it, in order to be completely alone in that interior silence in which its hidden life secretly expands.

It is sufficient for us to turn aside from all that draws us out of ourselves, to feel that everything within us is moving in the direction in which our deepest aspirations draw us. This is simply an inward silence which is a mute acceptance of grace. It is not one particular act, but a consent of the whole soul to what God is working in us, the soul's deep-rooted aherence to what is being wrought in its hidden depths—something that lies below its more superficial activities and with which it must be faithful to keep contact.

It is an interior silence in which we simply remain open to the hidden action of grace, and it is this hidden action of grace which gradually fosters dispositions which we are astonished to find in ourselves without knowing how they came to be there.

It is grace that awakens in us that interior aspiration which, however secret its action, keeps us as it were naturally turned towards God, so long as we do not allow ourselves to be positively distracted by some thought or preoccupation which would draw us elsewhere.

This is an interior silence in which we dwell, even though we seem to find nothing there, because we know intuitively that it conceals the only thing that matters for us—a thing which, even when hidden, none the less allows its presence to be sensed.

It is a silence in which we cannot remain recollected without feeling inwardly strengthened, as though we were receiving hidden nourishment. However empty this silence may appear, we return to it so to speak instinctively, it is to this that we are attracted and there and there alone do we feel at peace. It is an interior silence in which we feel we are in God's hands, at his disposal—and that he is free to act as he pleases in us.

It is an inward silence in which we have learnt to recognize God's presence, however hidden it may be and even if it does not manifest itself by any particular sign. The true sign of God's presence is not some passing impression experienced in prayer, but rather the soul's entire life, which is inexplicable without it.

It is an interior silence in which the soul is at peace, with that almost imperceptible difference in its attitude which makes it realize that its peace comes not from any confidence in itself but from the feeling that it is in God's hands.

It is a simple expectation, but in this expectation there

is an offering—we offer ourselves to the gift of grace. For, with God, to offer oneself is to offer oneself to his gifts, to seek to enter into the stream of his life which is wholly loving and giving.

It is a silence which expresses the humble prayer of a truly detached soul which no longer has anything of its own and of which God can dispose as he pleases.

This prayer is utterly detached and establishes the soul in a complete interior detachment which finds expression even in the renunciation of external things.

VI

GOD'S PRESENCE

This interior silence is nothing but a very simple disposition of the will, the result of the whole work of grace in the soul, a disposition which, as soon as we become recollected, we realize is present.

It is a simple silence—we have only to be completely alone to find ourselves with God. We can no longer be separated from him and cannot leave him except by leaving ourselves.

We cannot reflect on ourselves without seeing that everything in us presupposes the presence of God, that nothing subsists in us except through him, that our deepest aspirations are completely filled with him.

We feel that all we see within us presupposes something else, which remains hidden.

The simple consciousness we have of self is wholly filled with God, with the peace which we find in him. We can see ourselves only in him, since our whole life is an aspiration towards him.

Even when we find only emptiness within ourselves, we feel that this void is not what it would be if God were absent. It is enough for us to think of what God's absence would mean to us for the simple peace we enjoy to seem an adequate sign of his presence.

God is never wholly absent—the soul is never wholly what it would be if he were not there. We can always find within ourselves some sign of his presence which, however slight and scarcely perceptible it may be, is sufficient for us to be able to remain attentive to it.

The sign of God's presence is the interior atmosphere in which we find ourselves by reason of our fundamental orientation towards him, rather than any particular thought or feeling.

The thoughts with which we can occupy ourselves are not the whole of our prayer. The latter is made up of the resonances which such thoughts awaken in the soul under the influence of grace, and these resonances are not all perceptible.

There is an interior silence in which we can dwell peacefully, protected from the selfish preoccupations which can so easily stifle our thought and our very heart—such a silence, however empty of God it may appear, is actually full of God and is a prayer.

SPIRITUAL SOBRIETY

I

HIDDEN GRACE

We cannot have a true love of prayer and make it the dominant interest of our whole life except in so far as we love it, not for what we see in it but for all that is beyond and remains hidden from us.

Our prayer is not our work alone; God works with us. Thus it goes beyond the limits of our own activity, of all that is ours or becomes so in some sort from the fact that we become aware of it. This prayer lays us completely open to the hidden work of grace within us.

We must not behave as if grace only worked in us in the measure in which we are aware of it. The important thing is not so much to be aware of the action of grace as to keep ourselves responsive to it, to allow it to grow within us, however secretly. What is important is to content ourselves with a simple and general attraction to grace which is sufficient for our soul to remain touched by it and to come under its life-giving influence.

What is needed is a simple glance towards God in which is expressed our expectation of his grace and our awareness of being able to do nothing without it; a simple glance towards God, in which the soul opens itself to grace, so that grace may be free to do all that it pleases within it; a simple attentiveness to grace which spontaneously becomes submission, the entrusting of ourselves wholly to the hands of God.

We become aware of grace as of a reality which is in us and to which we must be wholly submissive—a reality whose presence can be known from very simple indications which we cannot define. We merely know that we should not be the same if there were not within us this reality that remains hidden from us.

All we have to do is to maintain an attitude of complete responsiveness, and remain fully open to the action of grace. It is enough for us to enter into contact with grace by means of the very least indication which is perceptible to us. We repeat, the very least indication—the action of grace can even be so secret that the soul has difficulty in discerning any indication of God's presence, which is yet sufficient to nourish it.

What the soul sees in itself is not its whole prayer, but merely an indication revealing to it the existence of the most hidden work accomplished in it by God.

To become aware of this prayer is not to enshrine it in our thoughts as a closed and limited whole, but to enter into contact with it as with a life which is overflowing on every side. To reduce our soul to what we can clearly see in it would be to mutilate it. We cannot reach to its depths but we can at least perceive enough to realize that it is deeper than our vision is able to penetrate.

The final thing that the soul will find in its hidden depths is the feeling of its dependence and this is a proof that, if it could penetrate a little further, immediately beyond it would find God. In the soul sanctified by grace, however, this feeling of dependence is the feeling of living by a gift that is entirely gratuitous, and that is why the presence which it allows us to glimpse is not that of an all-powerful master but of a love that is infinitely kind.

Since we live by a reality that is hidden within us and reached only through the darkness of faith, we should not be surprised if the sentiments which arise in us share in this darkness and if we can live by them almost without realizing the fact.

We should be willing to find nothing which we can confine within the limits of our own thoughts. What we are seeking is something simpler which we can glimpse only in its most secret recesses.

II

RESPONSIVENESS TO GRACE

We must learn to trust God and open our soul to him by an act of consent, allowing him to accomplish what he pleases in us without seeking to become aware of all he does. Our souls must be responsive, established in an interior disposition of acquiescence, of submission, which opens them to grace and enables grace to become active and exercise its hidden influence.

To transform our soul interiorly by the action of grace,

God waits only for our consent. He waits for it, desires it, listens to recognize the first sign we give him of it, even if it be a simple glance towards him, a word only half-spoken. We should thus turn towards him with a simplicity full of trust. We have only to offer ourselves to God as best we can, for him to make perfect this imperfect offering by taking possession of us with his grace.

Whether God seems to work within us or not matters little, provided we remain in the attitude of expectation and pure submissiveness which enables him to act in us if he pleases. If he seems to pay no attention to us when we thus offer ourselves to him and seems to ignore us, we must not allow ourselves to fall into the error of withholding our act of faith in his goodness.

It is our very helplessness that we should use to make a prayer of. To acknowledge this is to become aware of our absolute poverty. To accept it in simplicity is to consent to this absolute poverty, in an act of confidence in him from whom we must expect everything.

By the simple fact of accepting our helplessness peacefully, we put ourselves into God's hands and nothing else is needed than to feel that we are in his hands.

The more we abandon ourselves to God in simplicity in prayer, the better we understand that it is our whole life that we must abandon into his hands. This life belongs to him alone and we must leave him free to do what he pleases with it and appropriate nothing to ourselves.

III

SELF-STRIPPING

We live by the utter generosity of the gifts of God and we come to know how much everything in us is the work of his grace. Our whole happiness is to have nothing of our own. In utter simplicity we allow God to take our life in his hands and dispose of it as of something belonging to him. This is the simplicity and freedom of abandonment.

The action of grace becomes increasingly simple. It no longer needs to manifest its presence by perceptible signs, but can act very secretly in all its purity in the soul which is content to submit to it humbly in the simplicity of faith. That is why prayer becomes something very simple, very detached and in some sense very ordinary.

We simply hold ourselves open to the action of grace. This action of grace is something very secret and delicate which can pass almost unperceived. It is a life-giving influence, under which everything in us gradually becomes simpler, more peaceful, more submissive, more given. We feel that we are living in an atmosphere that is very calm and very pure. This is not a state which we can reach by our own efforts, but something we find within ourselves which can be perceived even in the simplest attitudes. All we have to do is to remain attentive to it. It is something we find within ourselves—and which remains obscure to us—and this is sufficient for us to realize that it is not our own but is a gift. That is all we need know for everything in us to merge increasingly into an attitude of humble thanksgiving, of confident and joyful submission, which is now our entire prayer.

If we live in the presence of the mystery of grace, our whole being falls into harmony with grace. Through the thoughts and feelings aroused in us by grace which we strive to maintain in ourselves, we gradually enter more deeply into a general disposition of detachment from self and complete belonging to God. The more perfect this interior disposition becomes, however, the less it requires such supports. It gradually detaches itself from them, until it is finally nothing more than a wholly natural, wholly spontaneous attitude of the will, by which the soul lives without adverting to it.

That is why, when our prayer becomes truly perfect, it becomes something completely simple and ordinary, and it is then that it is truly pure, the expression of a gift that is entirely spontaneous and with no return upon itself, a gift which is expressed naturally without having continually to struggle against contrary tendencies.

It is a simple, ordinary prayer, the attitude of a soul which knows itself to be in the hands of God and which quite naturally, as it were, without thinking of it allows him to dispose of it as he pleases. It is a tranquillity which is wholly simple, the fruit of abandonment, something hidden in the soul's innermost recesses, which pacifies everything in it; something which fills us to overflowing and to which we cleave with all our strength.

IV

THE GIFT OF SELF

This is a humble responsiveness which opens the soul to grace—not to some sensible grace which it might expect to experience in prayer, but to a hidden action of grace of which all we can see is that our whole life is transformed by it. We find that there is gradually being established in us an attitude of interior freedom, of simple and peaceful joy, a joy that is completely selfless, calm and full of kindliness towards all men. We feel happy, with a happiness which remains hidden from us, but which is for us the source of a peace which nothing can disturb.

It is a joy which lies dormant, but which awakens and becomes more intense when, on the occasion of some sacrifice that is demanded of us, we realize that we possess this joy which is wholly filled with the need of giving, of stripping self in order to have nothing more of our own and of being wholly abandoned in the hands of him who is making us so happy, who has given us all things and from whom we will to expect everything.

We feel all the more strongly that we have nothing of our own when we realize how much our very prayer—our most precious possession—is not our own. In prayer, indeed, we do nothing but strive to make ourselves wholly submissive, to put ourselves in a disposition which will enable God to accomplish the work of his grace in us freely. Our prayer is not our own, it is something completely given over into the hands of God. Why, then, should we not surrender all the rest? How could we still think of claiming anything as our own? We no longer have anything that is really ours. We expect everything from God.

Everything we have is at the disposal of anyone. Our life belongs to God and it is our joy to leave it in his hands, no longer to trouble about anything, since he alone can dispose of everything in our life at his good pleasure.

We can be simple just in so far as we no longer have anything of our own. In prayer we shall enjoy complete freedom in the measure in which we leave even our prayer in the hands of God as his possession and his alone. We shall enjoy a peace that nothing will be able to disturb in the measure in which we are wholly given to God and no longer have anything we seek to retain as our own possession. We should love to give everything—to forgive everything—for, to be able to live by the gifts of God, one must no longer have anything of one's own.

We strive to maintain towards everything the disposition in which we feel we are in harmony with the gift of grace and which will conduce to our greater growth in grace. We strive to avoid in our attitude towards external things, all that we feel to be in opposition to our interior attitude in the presence of grace. We reject every interior movement which, because it is bound up with self-assertion or egotistical demands, would form an obstacle to the humble and calm submission of a soul that no longer belongs to itself.

In the measure in which God takes possession of the soul in prayer, we shall understand what a stripping of self is involved in this belonging to him. We shall discern everything, both in our interior attitude and in our outward acts, that is contrary to this complete stripping of a soul that no longer belongs to itself. We shall see the exigencies of the true renunciation of self increasingly clearly. We shall understand what it is to be truly given.

This inward stripping is a disposition before God, a perfect suppleness in the presence of every manifestation of his will, but it demands of us the renunciation of what would deprive us of the freedom of a soul abandoned to the divine will because it would put self-will first.

The aim of our efforts of renunciation is to remove these resistances of our own will; wherever such resistance manifests itself, an effort must be made until it is broken down.

V

ASPIRING TOWARDS GOD

When there is no longer between the soul and God any self-assertion, any self-will, we feel ourselves united to God and can reach him directly, without any intermediary. By renouncing our own will, we can become really empty of self and wholly submissive, so that God may be free to do what he pleases with us. There is then no longer anything in us but this action of God, to which we are content to respond, even though it remain wholly secret.

The soul moves spontaneously whither its deepest aspiration draws it and finds peace there. The will moves not towards such and such an object which is presented to it, but where the deepest aspiration it feels in its inmost depths leads it. The will should acquiesce very simply in all the aspirations which the soul senses in a confused manner in its deepest being without the need to be explicitly aware of them. What is important is not to be aware of them but to respond to them.

What we discover in ourselves is primarly an aspiration towards God, and it is in this tendency towards him that we find a new and deeper knowledge of God. This aspiration is a desire, a call from God. We are, however, full of peace, as if this were already a possession. It is something hidden in our most secret recesses, but which penetrates us through and through and its influence may be glimpsed even in the simplest acts. It is an atmosphere in which we live.

Beyond all the thoughts and all the feelings through which something of this aspiration may be perceptible, is the hold of grace over the will, keeping it fixed on God. In simple terms, it is something which makes the disposition of the will simpler, deeper, more reliable. It is a clinging of the will to God, who takes possession of it wholly and leaves no room in it for anything else.

The will turns in simplicity towards that which it has

no need of knowledge in order to love, that which we find when we allow ourselves simply to be guided by the attraction of pure love which draws us we know not where. This attraction is purely in the will and through it we perceive that we are entering into contact with something we cannot find in any thought of our own, something that the will alone can attain and that it can only attain by detaching itself from all the rest.

VI

THE LIBERTY OF GRACE

What holds the soul back and encloses it within itself is egoism. A soul that is given to God is completely open and no longer feels it has any limits. It feels free to rise to God, who no longer seems to it unattainable. The selfish soul is shut up within itself and feels alone. The soul that is given to God is open and has the realization of a divine presence. The foundation of prayer is an aspiration which makes us move out from self and which we realize is opposed to any selfish movement which would turn us in upon ourselves.

We find our joy in a treasure that is not our own, and we are no longer satisfied with those lesser joys to which we can indeed lay claim but which are limited for that very reason. Not only do we expect everything from God as if we had confided our interests (though they would remain our own) to him, but we forget all our own concerns to live henceforward on that good which we expect from God alone, and which remains his alone—a good that remains divine and that we do not confine within our own narrow limits when we make it our own. The sole obstacle between God and us is ourselves. When we cannot find God within ourselves, it is because we come up against something in which we find self. When eventually we do find him, everything within us effaces itself before him. It is thus by an act of renunciation that we can best become aware of the presence of God within us, an act of that effacement of the whole of ourselves which is the token of his presence.

VII

GOD ALONE

Neither thought nor will can be empty of the things of this world unless they are full of God. If the mind can freely turn aside from every human thought, this is the sign that the soul can live without human consolation because its whole joy is in God. To think of God and God alone is to delight in nothing but him. The effort to think only of him is an effort to love him alone. To strive to turn our glance away from the things of this world to keep it fixed on God is to make an effort to renounce the world. If we are afraid of finding too much pleasure in some human joy, the simplest way of purifying our hearts is simply to turn our gaze away. It is by renouncing the joy of thinking of what we love too much that we shall gradually detach our heart from it.

If we want God to be all in all for us, our heart should always be where we will our treasure to be.

PEACE AND CONFIDENCE

I

PURE PRAYER

PURE PRAYER may be said to be a simple consent, by which we place ourselves under the influence of grace, whose action within us surpasses all we can imagine; or again, the awareness of this grace, in its character of a hidden thing, before which we feel our poverty and become humbler and more submissive—and in its character of a thing freely given, by which we cannot live without experiencing the desire to be utterly stripped of self and wholly given, the desire for that complete responsiveness of a soul in which the resistance of selfishness and the hardness of self-assertion have been effaced.

It is sufficient for us to enter into contact—however slightly—'by a simple desire of the heart', with the action of grace within ourselves. This contact may be a simple attention to God, which must be blended with humility, if we are truly to experience the touch of grace. All that is humble is prayer.

It is the disposition of utter self-surrender of a soul truly stripped of itself, of a soul that is detached and wholly given to God.

The soul must be humble and humility means no longer to count anything as one's own.

The most rewarding prayer for the soul is that in which it feels itself poorest—a poor prayer that must be left in its poverty, which is its purity. When we are conscious of our poverty, we should simply offer this poverty to God. All that we want to express to God can be expressed in this simple offering.

Our attitude should be that of inward calm and simplicity, the peace that is the fruit of humility, of the spirit of submission. It should be a simple glance towards God, which is an act of faith and abandonment. Our knowledge that we are in the hands of God should suffice.

God has taken possession of us, we are conscious of living in his will. All that comes from us is pure responsiveness and adherence to God. We simply acquiesce in God's taking possession of us. We do not give ourselves to him, we realize that we are wholly his.

II

THE WORK OF GRACE

We should not seek to enter immediately into contact with grace, as if we could attain this by our own efforts, but allow it to work gently in us and imperceptibly set us, under its secret influence, in a new atmosphere.

The work of grace that is accomplished in us is a work of inward transformation which takes place of itself, gradually, without our always being fully aware of it, and to which we have only to surrender ourselves calmly.

Our progress in all those inward dispositions which enable us to live the life of grace more fully is gradual, and we do not consciously advert to them in thought because we put them into practice by our humble acceptance of the obscure workings of grace. By submitting ourselves very simply to the work of grace which is being accomplished in us, we learn no longer to have any will of our own, no longer to live by our own will but by that of God.

We should will whatever God wills and will nothing apart from his will for us. We should not choose the best of our desires, but abandon them all without exception to allow God to dispose of us as he pleases.

The union of our will with that of God should be simple. The simpler it is the more perfect it is, for the simpler it is, the more it expresses the entire effacement of our will before God's will.

Our prayer should be wholly open to grace and quite simple. By this very simplicity we offer ourselves to grace, that it may work in us as it pleases. By this very simplicity grace can make the soul understand what is pleasing to God.

What we desire, and love, is to be at God's free

disposal. That is our whole prayer and our whole joy. A soul who, aware that it can do nothing of itself, leaves God free to act in it as he pleases, is simple.

We do not need to express our interior dispositions explicitly. It is sufficient for us to live very simply in the interior atmosphere which is the fruit of those dispositions, and which has no explanation without them. This is an atmosphere made up of a simplicity and liberty which we should not enjoy if we were not wholly surrendered to God—and which is thus a prayer—but which is something so natural and spontaneous that we are not aware that we are praying. It is an interior disposition that is very simple, but which can only be the achievement of a soul given to God, a disposition whose different aspects are so closely linked together that it is found in its entirety in each one of them.

For the expression of these interior dispositions in prayer, it is not necessary for them to be actually present to our mind in a precise manner—it is sufficient that there should be in our interior attitude something which presupposes these habitual dispositions and that something of them should come to the surface however slightly.

III

SECRET LIFE

There is an inner atmosphere in the depths of which the action of grace can be sensed. As soon as by simply keeping interior silence we place ourselves in this atmosphere, we feel ourselves in touch with God who works in our innermost recesses.

However simply we may come into touch with the inward realities, the depths of such realities are lost in God. It is with God that we have come into touch.

God's work in us is effected in secret, we know nothing of its hidden riches which extend beyond our consciousness. They may, however, be glimpsed in each of our actions which becomes as it were animated with a new life. In each of these acts, in a very simple way, we feel the contact of this life though we should gain nothing by seeking for a more precise experience of it. It is enough for us to enter into contact with this life, however secretly it may be. It is in living by it very simply that we live by it truly, as by a gift of God.

Even if we do not feel the touch of grace, we know that all that is required for this contact to establish itself is simply to hold ourselves open to the action of grace in us, by an attitude of responsiveness.

We should pray with our whole being, without even being aware that we are praying. The atmosphere in which we live is transformed by the imperceptible presence of grace, everything in us is penetrated with grace and betrays its secret influence, without our even suspecting it.

Of such a soul God has taken possession, taken it into his hands. It is nothing more than that—a thing in the hands of God. It is he who acts in it as he pleases. It is a soul that no longer belongs to itself in anything but belongs wholly to God from whom all its initiative comes. It is he who has taken possession of the soul by his grace, because he willed it to be wholly his.

There is a liberty of grace—the freedom of a soul which lives by God's free gift, which no longer has anything of its own or anything to claim as its own. It passes through all things and looks at all that surrounds it with a look of kindly charity which nothing can disturb.

For us to live in the joy of a very simple belonging to God, it is sufficient to express our belonging to him, in his presence, by our whole attitude, without even thinking of it, almost without knowing it.

In a word, there is then in us something simple and peaceful, which is the sign that we are detached and stripped of self, wholly surrendered into the hands of God. This is simply a state of inward peace, which seems to be something absolute, against which nothing can prevail because its foundation is God.

We live by hidden realities. Not only is our awareness of them obscure, but the very way in which we become aware of them and realize that we are living by them. We keep a certain contact in some way with these realities hidden within us, sometimes almost without realizing that we do so. Then everything in us is ready to turn towards God at the slightest movement it makes towards him, everything in us which is stirred into life, almost unconsciously, by a simple glance towards God.

IV

PEACE

It is not necessary that we should find God or feel him present, it is sufficient for us to seek him. It is sufficient for us to be turned towards him in some way or another, in expectation. It is sufficient that our whole attitude should express the desire for and expectation of grace.

This is sufficient to open us to grace, offering ourselves to its workings and sufficient for us to find ourselves in an atmosphere of wholly simple and utterly pure joy.

There is a certain depth in this simple cleaving to God which is only possible if we have understood and experienced how utterly we can do nothing and are nothing without him; how we receive everything from him, depend entirely on him and are wholly his. We must be content no longer to have anything of our own, because we know that it is sufficient for us to find ourselves wholly surrendered to God, so that he may accomplish in us what he pleases.

The simpler the prayer, the more full of trust it is. It should resolve itself into nothing but an act of confidence.

We turn to God very simply, by a mere desire. We have only to begin to turn towards him for him to take possession of us as we thus offer ourselves to him.

The most perfect act of love is confidence, faith. It is in the act of faith, of absolute confidence, that the genuine gift of self is realized. Of our whole life we should make an act of faith.

Abandonment. We realize that we belong to God, and should allow him to dispose of us as he pleases, and there is a feeling of security because we are in his hands.

Each one of our anxieties ought to be to us an occasion of renewing this act of abandonment in which we shall lose sight of the anxiety, for our only care will be that of remaining in God's hands, and that he may accomplish his will in us.

To love God is to find in him our peace.

To love God is to let ourselves be loved by him.

It is sufficient for us to be simply ourselves before God, with all that is the fruit of his grace in us—all that grace accomplishes in us, with which we enter into contact in some degree by the impression of peace, of interior liberty which itself is the fruit of grace.

The whole work of grace in the soul is manifest in this inward peace, in everything that gives it its distinctive attraction, its purity and delicacy.

The sign that this peace really comes from God is that

nothing can trouble it. It is something deeper than any disburbance. It is a peace that is based on the realization that we belong wholly to God.

We have a need of God but one that is deep and calm. It is impossible to say whether it is an aspiration towards him or the joy of being united to him. Every aspiration and every desire that awakens in the soul is satisfied in advance.

To put it simply we enjoy the happiness we find in God. It is a happiness that we do not always feel and yet we realize that we are never deprived of it. We are never without fundamental happiness. There is something austere and detached about our happiness, but this very austerity gives it an impression of plentitude. In an act of faith in him from whom we receive it, we give ourselves up to this happiness and know no other.

We should make this act of the love of God and desire to receive happiness from his hands alone, seeking no joy which we might try to procure ourselves because we ourselves desired it, and which he would not have given us.

The fruit of the love of God is a need of entire submission, a need of forgetfulness, of self-effacement, of total humility.

A soul who loves is humble. It does not need to have attention paid to it; any attention that was focussed on self has disappeared in the need to be wholly occupied with him whom it loves.

V

CONFIDENCE

Our will does not have to submit, it has only to offer its desire of submission. The divine will responds to its appeal and draws it to itself.

Its disposition should be one of entire belonging to God and the remitting of itself into his hands. This is only a poor rough outline of what the soul's attitude should be in his presence—but it knows this and its offering is made accordingly. It knows that its offering is addressed to a living God. It is in him will be found the force that is drawing the soul and that comes to strengthen the least movement that it tries to make towards him. The submission of a soul that realizes that everything in it comes from God and belongs to him, that feels itself wholly his, should be entire.

At the centre of our life is not only our love for God, it is primarily God's love for us. If our love is able to have some value, it is because, being a response to this divine love, it becomes one with it.

Our response to God's love is confidence, an act of total faith—to leave everything open to that love, at God's disposal, so that he may do in us what he pleases; and this not only because we know that he wills our good, but because we know that our only good is to be entirely surrendered to him—that everything in us is his and that he may dispose of us as he pleases.

To love only God's will in our regard is an act of confidence, and this act of confidence contains a gift of self without reserve.

We should love God's will—his will as regards ourselves personally—as the very expression of his love for us. We should welcome it with love and a love that is confident, and should delight to dwell in it.

To have a will of our own, to want something by an act of our own will, is an act of pride and is an infidelity and lack of confidence towards God's love. It is to want to take back into our own hands what is in the hands of God and entrusted to his love.

Our attitude should simply be that of a soul which has put all its faith in God and wants to keep it loyally for him. It belongs to him, it is his. There is the sense of a personal link with God, of a duty of personal fidelity towards him.

Our submission should be entire. What constitutes the depth of this submission is that it is a submission to love. Through it we open ourselves to the love of God. That is why the mystery of that love is reflected in us, with all its richness.

This belonging to God is something much more intimate than that which should be ours from the fact that we are his creatures—a belonging based on the far deeper mystery of grace. This belonging to God and dependence on him, which remains a mystery for the soul, but in which it finds its joy and rest, should be entire.

Before the will of God which is wholly love, submission and confidence are one and the same thing—and should be sufficiently whole-hearted to be an act of adoration in the presence of the infinite perfection of this divine will, of this divine love.

There must be a trust in God which is primarily submission and recognition of the sovereign dominion over us of God who is love, and a deep need of God which is the need of belonging to him without reserve.

We feel ourselves to be in God's hands and that suffices us. In all things he finds us accepting his will for us in each particular circumstance.

There is a peace and absolute security—the peace of a soul whom God has taken into his hands, in whom he accomplishes his will—peace in the love of this divine will.

Our submission is, then, complete trust, because it is utter love.

It is all that makes the will's adherence to God deeper and is expressed in the depth, the absoluteness of this adherence, which is a simple cleaving to what is most intimate to the will and most firmly rooted in it.

To put it briefly, all we need is a few very simple interior dispositions. As the action of grace becomes deeper, such dispositions become purer, more selfless, truer.

VI

SUBMISSIVENESS

Our whole life of prayer is based on the fact that we are living by a life which is a free gift of God, a participation in his life which is all giving and generosity.

The interior dispositions which are expressed in prayer are those which are in harmony with this life of grace—those which it inspires in us, towards which it moves us as it were instinctively—and which favour its growth in us.

A soul stripped of itself is simple and free—with a simplicity that is completely pure but wholly penetrated with sweetness. Such a soul is at peace and full of kindness.

These dispositions are expressed in our simple silence in the presence of God. They are expressed by the whole of ourselves and our whole attitude, and, too, by our attitude in the presence of our neighbour.

The perfect simplicity of a soul entirely ruled by grace, who lives by grace as it were naturally and spontaneously, almost without needing to think of it, can only be the result of a long and deep work of grace in us.

We should not then be afraid to express our feelings

in prayer in a more explicit, more precise manner when we feel that it is helpful and profitable to do so. What is important is to express our feelings to God as simply and sincerely as possible, that is, as naturally and spontaneously as possible.

To act thus, to try to pray simply as God invites us at a particular moment—in the way which best helps us to find him—is to remain in an attitude of humble submissiveness. The whole perfection of prayer is to express to God in one way or another this humble submission which opens the soul to grace, enabling grace to work in us as it pleases.

To pray is to lay ourselves open to grace, to receive it as a gift from God which remains his possession and his alone; to receive it with that disposition of humility and simplicity which corresponds to the delicate purity of this gift so freely bestowed.

What our response to grace, which our prayer seeks to express, ought to be is shown to us by our Lady in the mystery of her Annunciation. How simply she received the most unheard of gift—the announcement of the Incarnation, accompanied by the offer of the divine Motherhood. And what humility there is in that perfect simplicity : God is the master of his gifts, it is not for us to put forward conditions and objections, even were they objections coming from the realization of our unworthiness, but only to efface ourselves in submission—'Behold the handmaid of the Lord'.

Our Lady gives us the purest example of this total effacement.

As she received Christ, in whom all grace is offered to us, so ought we to try to receive this gift of grace, through which we are incorporated into Christ and live in him.